SRI DAMODAR LILA

Sri Srimad Radha Govinda Das Goswami

ISKCON
Bhagavata Mahavidyalaya
Publications

Readers interested in the subject matter of this book are invited to correspond with the Publisher. Email : ibmpublications@gmail. com

ISKCON Bhagavata Mahavidyalaya Publications
Gopinath Seva Dham, Opp Vaishnavo Devi Temple,
Vrindavan, Mathura281121.
A Division of
International Society for Krishna Consciousness
Hare Krishna Land, Juhu, Mumbai 400049.
Published by Buuks.

Although great care has been taken in compiling this book, some errors may have crept in. We humbly request our gentle readers to kindly forgive any inadvertent discrepancies. Please inform us of any observed errors so that we may amend them in our next edition.

—Publishers

Śrī Śrī Guru-Gaurāṅgau Jayataḥ

Sri Damodar Lila

tām ātta-yaṣṭiṁ prasamīkṣya satvaras
tato 'varuhyāpasasāra bhītavat
gopy anvadhāvan na yam āpa yogināṁ
kṣamaṁ praveṣṭuṁ tapaseritaṁ manaḥ

— *Bhāg*. 10. 9. 9

When Lord Sri Krishna saw His Mother, stick in hand, He very quickly got down from the top of the mortar and began to flee as if very much afraid. Although yogis try to capture Him as *Paramātmā* by meditation, desiring to enter into the effulgence of the Lord with great austerities and penances, they fail to reach Him. But Mother Yashoda, thinking that same Personality of Godhead, Krishna, to be her son, began chasing Krishna to catch Him.

Acknowledgements

Many thanks to all the devotees who worked hard to produce this book:

Editor : Brajsunder Das
Copy Editor : Isha Prakash Das
Saṅskrit Editor : Vrajsevika Devi Dasi
Translated : Sri Nilmani Das
Navanitika Devi Dasi
Assitance : Harilila Dasi, Damayanti Devi Dasi
Bhavamayi Devi Dasi, Daivisakti Devi Dasi
Cover Design: Ananda Rupa Das

ARTISTS

Front cover page: Damodar Lila painting © by Bhaktivedanta Book Trust.
Other paintings inside book by Kim Waters Murray.
Her website: www. kimwatersart. net

First printing, January 2012 – 3,000 copies
Second printing, October 2019 – Print on demand through BUUKS.com

Dedicated to
His Divine Grace
A. C. Bhaktivedanta Swami Prabhupada
Founder-*Ācārya* of the
International Society for Krishna Consciousness

TABLE OF CONTENTS

Mangalacarana........................ 1

Sri Damodar Lila........................ 4

The Glories of Sri Damodar............. 39
(Sri Damodarastak)
Glossary....................... 45

Index to songs and verses.... 50

Mangalacharana

oṁ ajñāna-timirāndhasya jñānāñjana-śalākayā
cakṣur unmīlitaṁ yena tasmai śrī-gurave namaḥ

I was born in the darkest ignorance, and my spiritual master opened my eyes with the torch of knowledge. I offer my respectful obeisances unto him.

śrī-caitanya-mano-'bhīṣṭaṁ sthāpitaṁ yena bhū-tale
svayaṁ rūpaḥ kadā mahyaṁ dadāti sva-padāntikam

When will Srila Rupa Goswami Prabhupada, who has established within this material world the mission to fulfill the desire of Lord Chaitanya, give me shelter under his lotus feet?

vande 'haṁ śrī-guroḥ śrī-yuta-pada-kamalaṁ śrī-gurūn vaiṣṇavāṁś ca
śrī-rūpaṁ sāgrajātaṁ saha-gaṇa-raghunāthānvitaṁ taṁ sa-jīvam
sādvaitaṁ sāvadhūtaṁ parijana-sahitaṁ kṛṣṇa-caitanya-devaṁ
śrī-rādhā- kṛṣṇa –pādān saha-gaṇa-lalitā-śrī-viśākhānvitāṁś ca

I offer my respectful obeisances unto the lotus feet of my spiritual master and unto the feet of all *vaiṣṇavas*, I offer my respectful obeisances unto the lotus feet of Srila Rupa Goswami along with his elder brother Sanatana Goswami, as well as Raghunatha Das Goswami and Raghunatha Bhatta, Gopala Bhatta, and Srila Jiva Goswami. I offer my respectful obeisances to Lord Sri Krishna Chaitanya and Lord Nityananda along with Adwaita Acharya, Gadadhara, Srivas, and other associates. I offer my respectful obeisances to Srimati Radharani and Sri Krishna along with Their associates Sri Lalita and Vishakha.

he kṛṣṇa karuṇā-sindho dīna-bandho jagat-pate
gopeśa gopīkā-kānta rādhā-kānta namo 'stu te

O my dear Krishna, O ocean of mercy, You are the friend of the distressed and the source of creation. You are the master of the gopis and the lover of Radharani. I offer my respectful obeisances unto You.

tapta-kāñcana-gaurāṅgi rādhe vṛndāvaneśvari
vṛṣabhānu-sute devi praṇamami hari-priye

I offer my respects to Radharani, whose bodily complexion is like molten gold and who is the Queen of Vrindavan. You are the daughter of King Vrishabhanu, and You are very dear to Lord Krishna.

vāñchā-kalpatarubhyaś ca kṛpā-sindhubhya eva ca
patitānāṁ pāvanebhyo vaiṣṇavebhyo namo namaḥ

I offer my respectful obeisances unto all the *vaiṣṇava* devotees of the Lord. They can fulfill the desires of everyone, just like desire trees, and they are full of compassion for the fallen souls.

jaya śrī-kṛṣṇa –caitanya prabhu-nityānanda
śrī-advaita gadādhara śrīvāsādi-gaura-bhakta-vṛnda

I offer my obeisances to Sri Krishna Chaitanya, Prabhu Nityananda, Sri Adwaita, Gadadhar, Srivas and all others in the line of devotion.

hare kṛṣṇa hare kṛṣṇa kṛṣṇa kṛṣṇa hare hare
hare rāma hare rāma rāma rāma hare hare

śrī-śuka uvāca
ekadā gṛha-dāsīṣu yaśodā nanda-gehinī
karmantara-niyuktāsu nirmamantha svayaṁ dadhi

— *Bhāg.* 10. 9. 1

One time, on the day of *dīpāvalī*, Mother Yashoda wondered why her son was stealing *mākhan* from other people's houses. She thought, "Maybe Krishna does not like the *mākhan* in my house. If this is the case, then today I will make the *mākhan* myself."

In Mother Yashoda's house, there were many maidservants who milked the cows, made yogurt and *mākhan* and did various other household duties. Nanda Maharaja had 900,000 cows. Most of these cows produced milk which would then be made into yogurt and *mākhan*. This was a lot of work and they needed many maidservants. In addition to these, there were other more intimate maidservants who helped Mother Yashoda look after Krishna. These maidservants were very conscientious and made yogurt and *mākhan* under the personal direction of Mother Yashoda for the pleasure of her dear son Krishna.

Mother Yashoda started getting many complaints from all the other gopis about Krishna stealing *mākhan* from their houses, breaking pots and generally wreaking havoc. Because of this, she had doubts about the *mākhan* in her house. She thought, "May be our yogurt is not very good or, our *mākhan* is not

Gopis Complain to Mother Yasoda About Damodara's Mischief

coming out perfectly? Otherwise, why would Krishna go to other gopis houses to steal what was readily available at home?" She did not realize that Krishna went because of the *premā* that the other gopis had, not simply to steal their *mākhan*. Mother Yashoda did not realize this and therefore she had doubts about what she was giving to Krishna. Because of this doubt she decided that she would make the yogurt with her own hands and churn it into the best *mākhan* that Krishna had ever tasted. She wanted to do this every day to stop Krishna from stealing.

Mother Yashoda is a queen and churning yogurt is actually not appropriate for a queen. Yet, in order to completely satisfy Krishna, one day she started churning the yogurt herself, *nirmamantha svayaṁ dadhi.*

In Sanskrit, *dā* means time. It is used in words like *sarvadā, ekadā, yadā, kadā. Ekadā* means "at one time", *yada* means "at some time", *kadā* means "at which time", and *sarvadā* means "at all times". Here Sukadeva Goswami says: "*Ekadā* (At one time), Mother Yashoda started to churn the yogurt." Then what did the intimate maidservants do now that their usual duties had been taken up by Mother Yashoda? *Karmantara-niyuktāsu*, she engaged them in other services. Mother Yashoda directed them to attend other household duties, saying that she herself would extract the *mākhan* for Krishna. The poor maidservants were very sincere in their duties and actually made very tasty *mākhan*. However, because Mother Yashoda was doubtful of the quality of their *mākhan*, she engaged them elsewhere and took it upon herself to make *mākhan* for Krishna.

Ekadā here refers to the day of *dīpāvalī* in the month of *kārtika*. This was the day Mother Yashoda bound Krishna. Many of Sri Krishna's prominent *līlās* occurred in *śarad kāla* or *kārtika*. Some examples are *rāsa-līlās*, *govardhan līlās* and *damodar līlā*. To stop Sri Krishna from stealing and to keep Him happy at home, Mother Yashoda started to churn yogurt. While doing so, she sang the glories of Sri Krishna's childhood pastimes.

yāni yānīha gītāni tad-bāla-caritāni ca
dadhi-nirmanthane kāle smarantī tāny agāyata

— *Bhāg.* 10. 9. 2

Tad-bāla-caritāni ca. Mother Yashoda sang about the *līlās* which Krishna had performed. She sang about the deliverance of Putana, Aghasura, Shakatasura and Trnavarta, the *līlā* of Krishna learning how to walk, Krishna eating *mākhan*, and other *līlās* He had performed. Mother Yashoda sang spontaneously as these memories arose in her heart. As she remembered these wonderful pastimes, she became naturally joyful. When was she singing? *dadhi-nirmanthane kale-* Mother Yashoda was singing Krishna's pastimes at the time of churning the *dadhi*, yogurt.

Sukadeva Goswami continues to describe this wonderful picture.

kṣaumaṁ vāsaḥ pṛthu-kaṭi-taṭe bibhratī sūtra-naddhaṁ
putra-sneha-snuta-kuca-yugaṁ jāta-kampaṁ ca subhrūḥ
rajjv-ākarṣa-śrama-bhuja-calat-kaṅkaṇau kuṇḍale ca
svinnaṁ vaktraṁ kabara-vigalan-malatī nirmamantha

— *Bhāg.* 10. 9. 3

First of all he says *kṣaumaṁ vāsaḥ pṛthu-kaṭi-taṭe bibhratī. Kṣaumaṁ* means, saffron yellow. Mother Yashoda was wearing a saffron yellow sari, *sūtranaddhaṁ*, tied tightly on her hips with a belt. Dressed in this way, Yashoda was fully prepared to perform this *sevā*. This was very early in the morning, before sunrise, at the time called *maṅgala* or *bhor*. At this time, Mother Yashoda had risen and was working hard, thinking, "Before Krishna wakes up, let me extract the *mākhan* so that I can feed Him. Why was she wearing a saffron yellow sari? It is said that saffron is a very pure color so by wearing that, she could perform this *sevā* perfectly, in all detail.

Putra-sneha-snuta-kuca-yugaṁ jāta-kampaṁ ca subhrūḥ. Mother Yashoda's breasts, were moving from the motion of the churning rod and because of *putra-sneha,* unalloyed love for her son Krishna, milk was flowing. Why was the milk flowing from her breasts? It is said that in the transcendental world everything is conscious. This is just the opposite of the material world, where almost everything is insentient. Mother Yashoda's milk, being of transcendental nature, was thinking, "Today Mother Yashoda is working hard to extract the *mākhan* and will feed it to Krishna. Therefore He will eat the *mākhan* and become fully satisfied. He will not drink me. Being deprived of Krishna's service, what then will become of me?" Thinking in this way, the milk was flowing out from her breasts.

With the whole of her being, Mother Yashoda was churning the yogurt. As she was pulling the rope of the churning rod, her golden bangles were shaking and making a sweet sound— "*jhan jhan jhan*" Her earrings shook and jingled harmoniously. Then, her ankle bells and the golden belt around her waist also joined in, creating a beautiful melodious sound. It was as if an expert *karatāla* player was playing. As she was churning the yogurt, the churning rod went "*gharad gharad gharad*", sounding like an expert *mṛdaṅga* player. In this way, Mother Yashoda had full musical accompaniment as she continued to sing about Krishna's glorious childhood pastimes.

She became so absorbed in this churning that she completely forgot herself and lost awareness of her own body. *Svinnaṁ vaktraṁ*, on her forehead and over her face there was perspiration which made her look even more beautiful. It was as if she had never churned yogurt so intensely before. In this way she was churning yogurt. When someone works hard and perspires, his beauty and charm increases, especially when engaged in performing devotional service. *Kabara-vigalan-malatī nirmamantha*, in her hair she was wearing a garland made of *malati* flowers. Even the *malati* flowers from this garland were falling to the ground, due to her intense endeavor.

In this way she was *nirmamantha*, churning the yogurt. Her hands and body were engaged in this intensive labour, *pariśrama*, to make the *mākhan*. Her tongue was singing the glories and pastimes of Krishna. Her ears were engaged in hearing those songs. And her mind was remembering and meditating on how she would make the *mākhan* to feed Krishna. This is the state of a perfect devotee, fully engaging mind, body and intelligence in the service of Krishna.

Many *ācāryas* have given their realizations on this pastime. Why were her bangles making a wonderful sound, *"jhan jhan jhan"*? In the transcendental world even the bangles are conscious, so the bangles were thinking, "Today we are so fortunate to be on the hands of Mother Yashoda, who are engaged in Krishna's *sevā*." They were singing out of joy and congratulating her. In reality our hands do not become beautiful simply by wearing golden jewelry; our hands can only be considered beautiful if we engage them in the service of the Supreme Lord. And her earrings were also moving back and forth as if jumping out of joy. They too were thinking, "Today we are fortunate to be on the ears that are engaged in hearing the glories of Krishna-on the ears of one who is engaged in Krishna's service." Her *malati* flowers were falling to the ground. Why was that? It was because the flowers were thinking, "Today *Mā* is engaged in Krishna's service and hence we do not belong on her head, but at her feet instead."

Mother Yashoda is fully and joyfully absorbed in this *dadhi-manthan sevā*, the churning of yogurt into *mākhan*. Hearing Mother Yashoda's voice and the melodious sounds of the *dadhi-manthan*, yogurt being churned, Krishna woke up earlier than usual.

tāṁ stanya-kāma āsādya mathnantīṁ jananīṁ hariḥ
gṛhītvā dadhi-manthānaṁ nyaṣedhat prītim āvahan

—*Bhāg*. 10. 9. 4

On this day, Krishna woke up earlier than usual. He was looking for His mother and thought, "Why is *Mā* not here with me on the bed?" Then He heard her singing in another room. He immediately thought, "What is wrong with her today? She is not worried about Me at all. She has left Me to start on her ordinary household duties."

When Krishna woke up, He became desirous to drink milk from her breasts, *stanya-kāma*. Children, even when they are babies, are very expert at getting the attention they want. When they don't get the attention they seek, they become very naughty. Usually when Krishna wakes up, Mother Yashoda is right there for him. She hugs Him, feeds Him, pampers Him, etc.

However today was different – Mother Yashoda was completely ignoring Him. Krishna thought, "Is this housework so important that she has to leave Me?" So He feigned crying, "Yaeee Yaeee". Rubbing His eyes with His hands, He started walking towards the room where He could hear her singing. He walked to where she was churning the yogurt *dadhi-manthānam* and looked up at her. However, Mother Yashoda did not notice that Krishna had come.

There is an important lesson here. When will Krishna come to us? Krishna will not come to

us when we are simply relaxing comfortably and thinking ourselves to be absorbed in meditation on Him. However, He feels greatly obliged to come to us when we are absorbed in devotional service, working hard and even perspiring for

Him. Krishna feels compelled to give us His darsana when we are so completely engaged in devotional service that we may not even notice His very presence.

Then baby Krishna looked around and wondered what He should do to get her attention. Thinking in this way, *gṛhītvā dadhi-manthānaṁ nyaṣedhat*, He caught hold of the churning rod and held it firmly with both hands as if applying the brake to a fast-moving bicycle. In this way, He was indicating to Mother Yashoda, "Stop! I need attention! Feed Me now!"

One *ācārya* has given his realization as to why Krishna stopped the churning. He stopped this churning to tell His mother, "All the *jñānīs* are constantly reading and analyzing the scriptures, trying to extract the essence, just churning, churning and churning. At last they may approach Me, for it is I who am the conclusion of all scriptures. Oh, My dear mother you are already with Me, so what is the use for all this churning?"

We can analyze the *Upaniṣads*, the *Vedas*, the *Purāṇas*, and the other Vedic scriptures. But what is their final conclusion? All the scriptures conclude that attaining Krishna is the highest goal of life. That Krishna is the son of Mother Yashoda. Why then would she have to do any churning? Why was she doing this unnecessary labour? For this reason, Krishna stopped His mother from churning the yogurt. Mother Yashoda then looked at Krishna but she did not

pick Him up. She waited to see what He would do next. Krishna caught hold of her arm with both hands, put one of His feet on the rim of the yogurt pot and climbed up onto her lap. Then He started drinking her breast milk. Mother Yashoda marveled at her son's cleverness in getting what he wanted all by himself. She was amazed and full of motherly pride, seeing how her little son Krishna had done all these things on His own.

tam aṅkam ārūḍham apāyayat stanaṁ
sneha-snutaṁ sa-smitam īkṣatī mukham
atṛptam utsṛjya javena sā yayāv
utsicyamane payasi tv adhiśrite

— *Bhāg.* 10. 9. 5

Upon realizing Krishna's desire, Mother Yashoda put aside all other work and focused on feeding her charming little child. Krishna smiled, which made Mother Yashoda very happy while she very proudly and pleasurably fed her endearing son. He also became very proud of Himself. He thought, "How smart I am. I stopped mother from her work and claimed My right." Thinking in this way, He smiled continuously, making His chubby cheeks more adorable.

As Krishna drank Mother Yashoda's breast milk, a transcendental competition began. Krishna's belly would not become satisfied and Mother Yashoda's milk would not stop flowing due to her intense affection. The milk was endeavoring to completely satisfy Krishna but Krishna can never be satiated with any amount of *premā*. So the milk continued to flow and Krishna continued to drink. In this way she continued feeding Him for a good long while, again becoming fully engrossed and losing all sense of time.

While Mother Yashoda was thus absorbed in feeding baby Krishna, something else caught her attention. On a nearby stove, the milk had started to boil over. Seeing this, Mother Yashoda quickly put Krishna down and ran to the stove to save the milk. In the transcendental realm milk is also conscious. The milk thought, "Why am I doing the *tapasya* (austerity) of tolerating this heat? If Krishna will not drink me but drink only Mother Yashoda's milk, then it is better for Me to commit suicide by jumping into the fire. If I cannot serve Krishna, then why should I live?" Thinking in this way, the milk started to boil over. In boiling over, the milk was also trying to get Mother Yashoda's attention.

Mother Yashoda then began thinking, "This is special milk from the Padmaganda cows. I must quickly save it as it is meant for Krishna!" Thinking like this, she put Krishna down and ran to save this milk.

In Vraja, Padmaganda cows are very special. Extraordinarily fragrant grasses were reserved for their grazing and their bodies emitted a wonderful lotus scent. There were only 100 such cows and they produced very special milk. Mother Yashoda had reserved some of this milk especially for Krishna.

As she ran to save that special milk, the milk, out of shame, stopped boiling over and resumed its normal state. The milk now started to think that it had committed a great offense by interrupting the loving exchange between Mother Yashoda and Krishna. The milk chided itself, "What have I done? Mother Yashoda was so

happy and joyful feeding Krishna and I impeded her devotional service. I am an offender."

Mother Yashoda reached the stove and put the milk aside. In the meantime, what was Krishna thinking?

sañjāta-kopaḥ sphuritāruṇādharaṁ
sandaśya dadbhir dadhi-mantha-bhājanam
bhittvā mṛṣāśrur dṛṣad-aśmanā raho
jaghāsa haiyaṅgavam antaraṁ gataḥ

—*Bhāg.* 10. 9. 6

Sañjāta-kopaḥ sphuritāruṇādharaṁ— Little Krishna now became angry. He thought,"How dare mother put Me aside while I am still drinking her milk? I am still hungry. Does she not care for Me at all? Just to save a little milk she throws Me aside and runs off. How dare she!" *sphuritāruṇādharaṁ*— His lips became swollen and red because He bit them with His small white teeth, "*Mā* does not care for Me at all. Who does she think she is, throwing Me aside just to save a little milk? I will show her. She will be sorry. I'll break everything in the house! I won't leave anything untouched."

Thinking in this way, Krishna looked around and saw a large spice grinding stone. With this stone He very cleverly struck the yogurt-churning pot. *Bhittvā mṛṣāśrur dṛṣad-aśmanā*— He aimed the stone to hit the bottom of the pot so that it would not make any sound which could alarm His mother. In this manner, He broke the pot which caused yogurt to spill all over the floor.

As Krishna hit the pot, He had false tears in his eyes (*mṛṣāśrur*). Being angry at Mother Yashoda's actions, Krishna began scheming and thinking of how to get back at her. In this way, He started to walk to a different room, looking for the previous day's *mākhan*. When He went, He walked through the yogurt that was spilt, making a sound - '*chub chub chub*'.

That *Bhagavān*, who in the form of Vaman deva spanned the whole universe with just three steps, was now walking through the spilt yogurt. He walked quietly so that His mother would not be able to hear the sound of His steps- '*chub chub chub*'. Child Krishna did not think that perhaps He should go around the yogurt. Krishna just walked right through, leaving cute footprints showing exactly where He, the cute *chor-mahārāja* (the great thief), had trod.

Even though there was fresh *mākhan* being made for Him, Krishna started as if to eat the previous day's *mākhan*. As He was doing so, He began thinking to Himself, "I will eat this *mākhan* and get sick. You will have to take me out of Vraja, to a hospital in Mathura where you will have to spend lots of money and take care of Me. I'll show you! Then you'll see. Then you'll be sorry!"

Krishna went into the other room, turned over the wooden grinding mortar, climbed on it and pretended to eat the old *mākhan*. He was actually not eating it; he just wanted to express to His mother, "See *Mā*, I was so hungry and without properly feeding Me, you just threw Me aside and left Me. What did you expect Me to do? You go and take care of your little milk, I'll take care of all this *mākhan* and yogurt; I won't leave you anything." Monkeys began to appear as if from nowhere and Krishna started feeding the *mākhan* to them, freely distributing and even throwing it in all directions.

uttārya gopī suśṛtaṁ payaḥ punaḥ
praviśya sandṛśya ca dadhy-amatrakam

bhagnaṁ vilokya sva-sutasya karma taj
jahāsa taṁ cāpi na tatra paśyatī

— *Bhāg*. 10. 9. 7

After rescuing the milk from the stove, Mother Yashoda returned and saw that the yogurt pot had been smashed to pieces. She immediately understood who had done this mischief. If Krishna had stayed where she had left Him, then she might have thought it was broken accidentally - something might have fallen on it, or some cat or animal might have knocked it over. However, because Krishna was not there, she concluded that it was His misbehavior.

Upon seeing the footprints, Mother Yashoda thought, "Krishna is guilty and He has run away." Actually, she was not really angry about the broken pot. She smiled to herself and thought, "Just see how clever my Krishna is. He broke this pot in such a way that I didn't hear a sound. This boy is so clever and yet so cheeky!" Therefore Mother Yashoda decided, "Today I have to punish Him because He has broken a pot. Who knows what He might do tomorrow? I must teach Him a lesson!" In this way, she followed His little footprints, hid behind a wall and looked around the corner to spy on Krishna.

ulūkhalāṅghrer upari vyavasthitaṁ
markāya kāmaṁ dadataṁ śici sthitam
haiyaṅgavaṁ caurya-viśaṅkitekṣaṇaṁ
nirīkṣya paścāt sutam āgamac chanaiḥ

— *Bhāg*. 10. 9. 8

Sukadeva Goswami says— *ulūkhalāṅghrer upari vyavasthitaṁ markāya kāmaṁ dadataṁ śici sthitam.* Mother Yashoda saw that Krishna had taken the grinding mortar, turned it upside down and sat on it. Krishna took the butter from the pots hanging from the rafters and began feeding it to the monkeys to their full satisfaction and great pleasure.

Mother Yashoda saw Krishna feeding the monkeys and like a thief afraid of getting caught, He was looking around with eyes full of fear. Krishna knew that Mother Yashoda would soon come looking for Him. She would certainly see the broken pot and if she caught Him, He would be beaten. *Nirīkṣya paścāt sutam āgamac chanaiḥ*— Seeing Krishna outside the house, Mother Yashoda crept up from behind Him to catch Him. However, Krishna saw her coming, carrying a stick in her hand!

tām ātta-yaṣṭiṁ prasamīkṣya satvaras
tato 'varuhyāpasasāra bhītavat
gopy anvadhāvan na yam āpa yogināṁ
kṣamaṁ praveṣṭuṁ tapaseritaṁ manaḥ

—*Bhāg.* 10. 9. 9

Tām ātta-yaṣṭiṁ prasamīkṣya— Krishna was afraid of the look on His mother's face and the stick in her hand. *Satvaras tato 'varuhyāpasasāra bhītavat*— Seeing this, Krishna jumped down from the grinding mortar. He fled, apprehensive of what she might do to Him. He thought, "If I am quick, she will not be able to catch Me and I will be saved. She will not be able to beat me."

In His heart, Krishna knew that He had been naughty and had done many things that He should not have done. He had broken Mother Yashoda's yogurt churning pot and fed *mākhan* to the monkeys. Normally *gṛhasthas* protect their

household paraphenalia and stored foodstuffs but Krishna was so naughty that He had fed their *mākhan* to the monkeys. It had taken a long time to make this *mākhan*. Krishna knew that He had been a bad boy. He knew that if Mother Yashoda caught Him, she would definitely beat Him.

Gopy anvadhāvan— Mother Yashoda did not want to let Krishna get away— she was determined to catch Him so she began to run after Him. This was the first time that such a *līlā* had taken place where Krishna was seen as at fault and His devotee was apparently angry at Him. Sukadeva Goswami next said— *na yam āpa yogināṁ kṣamaṁ praveṣṭuṁ tapaseritaṁ manaḥ*— the *yogīs*, whose minds have become purified by performing all types of austerities, and who can travel at the speed of the wind, cannot catch or attain Krishna. They are unable to do so in their minds even after thousands of years of meditation.

However, in this *līlās*, Mother Yashoda was running after that same unattainable Krishna- chasing Him with a stick in her hand. At first Krishna ran from room to room, with Mother Yashoda in chase. Then He left the house and ran into the streets of Gokul. Mother Yashoda resolved, "Today Krishna is not going to get away from me - wherever He goes, I will pursue Him." In this way she followed Him everywhere.

All the *vraja-vāsīs* looked on in amazement. They thought, "What is happening today? Usually there is so much affection between Krishna and Mother Yashoda - what could possibly have taken place?"

Being light and agile, Krishna was running in a zig-zag manner. He was running in and out of everyone's houses and Mother Yashoda was following Him. She remained determined to catch her mischievous son. However, Mother Yashoda was not used to running like this, so

she soon became tired and was perspiring.

After a long chase, Mother Yashoda finally caught Krishna and firmly grasped His right hand. With His left hand, Krishna wiped the tears from His eyes. Mother Yashoda addressed Him, *vānara-bandhu, manthanī sphotak*-"O friend of the monkeys, are these monkeys your relatives? Why are You feeding them so freely? O breaker of the yogurt pot, until now, I have not believed the complaints of the other *gopis*; but today I have caught You redhanded! Today You'll be severely punished. I will beat You!" She waved the stick at Krishna chiding Him, "Why did You break the pot? Tell me!"

Little Krishna was shaking in fear, crying and wiping His tears with His hands. As He wiped His tears, His eyeliner was smudged all over His face. Somehow, this made Him look even more beautiful. He cried again and again and pleaded, "*Mā*! Please let me go, I promise I'll never do this again. I promise. Please let Me go."

When Mother Yashoda saw that Krishna had become very frightened, she put the stick down. Krishna breathed a sigh of relief, thinking that perhaps the worst was over. He thought, "At least she won't hit me with a stick now. I will not get beaten."

This pastime demonstrates the uniqueness of Krishna's *vraja-līlā*. In no other incarnation does the Supreme Lord await judgment from anyone. Here, Krishna is guiltily standing in front of His mother, His fate completely in her hands. Mother Yashoda now has full jurisdiction to decide whether to punish, bind or release Krishna. This is the speciality of the parental affection, *vātsalya-bhāva* of Vraja where there the knowledge of Krishna's Godhood is covered. Sukadeva Goswami then says *arbhaka-vatsalā*—seeing the genuine fear in His eyes, Mother Yashoda put her stick down and contemplated on how else to discipline her mischievous son.

After discarding the stick, instead of beating Krishna, Mother Yashoda decided to tie Him up. She reasoned, "Krishna may run away to the bank of the Yamuna in an angry mood as He does when He gets upset. Sometimes when Krishna gets fed up and runs away, it takes me hours to find Him. I don't know what Krishna might do, especially now that He is in such a mood. If Krishna runs too far away, it may become very difficult to find Him or He may even get hurt. So let me tie Him up for a while. I can churn some more yogurt, make the *mākhan* and then I can return to pacify Him." With these thoughts, Mother Yashoda started to bind Krishna.

tyaktvā yaṣṭiṁ sutaṁ bhītaṁ vijñāyārbhaka-vatsalā
iyeṣa kila taṁ baddhuṁ dāmnātad-vīrya-kovidā

— *Bhāg*. 10. 9.12

What was Mother Yashoda's consciousness as she tied her son Krishna? *Atad-vīrya-kovidā*— Due to intense love for Krishna, Mother Yashoda was not aware of His position as the supremely powerful Personality of Godhead. She did not know that He was *svayam-bhagavān*, the original Supreme Personality of Godhead, therefore she endeavored to tie Him.

Svayam-bhagavān has an innate nature *(vīrya)*, which can also be known as *prabhāv*. Mother Yashoda was not aware of this. She did not know of the innate nature of her son. Krishna has no beginning, no end, no inside and no

outside. He is all-pervading. How can someone who possesses such qualities be tied up? It is impossible. However, Mother Yashoda simply saw Krishna as her son, so she endeavored to tie Him up.

In this regard Sukadeva Goswami says:

na cāntar na bahir yasya na pūrvaṁ nāpi cāparam
pūrvāparaṁ bahiś cāntar jagato yo jagac ca yaḥ

taṁ matvātmajam avyaktam martya-liṅgam adhokṣajam
gopīkolūkhale dāmnā babandha prākṛtaṁ yathā
— *Bhāg.* 10. 9. 13-14

The Supreme Personality of Godhead has no beginning and no end, no exterior and no interior, no front and no rear. In other words, He is all-pervading. Because He is not under the influence of the element of time, for Him there is no difference between past, present and future. He exists in His transcendental form at all times. Being absolute, beyond relativity, He is free from distinctions between cause and effect, although He is the cause and effect of everything. That unmanifested person, who is beyond the perception of the senses, had now appeared as a human child, and Mother Yashoda, considering Him her own ordinary child, bound Him to the wooden mortar with a rope.

How can such a personality ever be tied? Where would you start tying him up? However, Mother Yashoda succeeded in her attempt to bind Krishna. Why was that? Because of her intense love for Krishna, she believed Him simply to be her son, *ātmajam matvā*, an ordinary child. This intense love covered her knowledge that in fact, there is nothing inside or outside of Krishna. He has no beginning and no end. He is infinite and all-pervading. Her loving sentiments however predominated over Krishna's innate capacity or opulence.

When Mother Yashoda began to bind Krishna, an interesting phenomenon took place. No matter what length of rope she used, when she wanted to tie the knot on her lala's waist, it would always be short by the width of two fingers. Mother Yashoda became astonished. It was beyond her comprehension. Still she was determined to bind Krishna.

All of Krishna's energies had united and come to defend Him. They would not let anyone bind Krishna. His energies *vibhūti-śakti* and *satya-saṅkalpa-śakti* united and prevented Him from being tied. At first she used a ribbon from her hair. When this was too short she sent for all other cords and ropes from her house. In this way, she connected all the ropes available at home. Yet when the final knot was to be tied, she found that the rope was still two fingers too short.

One *ācārya* says that the reason why the ropes were always short was because Krishna was testing Mother Yashoda's determination. He wanted to see if she will give up trying to bind Him. Because Mother Yashoda's effort was not complete, Krishna's mercy was also not complete. Only upon seeing Mother Yashoda's fullest efforts, would Krishna extend His mercy.

ye yathā māṁ prapadyante
tāṁs tathaiva bhajāmy aham

—*Bg* 4. 11

In other words, Krishna waits for us to give our everything to Him before He gives us His mercy. This is why the binding rope was always short by two fingers. Krishna was demonstrating that He who is not bound in the beginning or the end cannot be bound in the middle either. Therefore, Mother Yashoda's attempts to bind Krishna at His waist (the middle portion) were never successful.

After using all the cords and ropes from her house, she sent for more from the other gopis houses. In the meantime, several other gopis gathered and looked at the scene in astonishment. They said to Yashoda, "Release Him. Let Him go! He is clearly not destined to be tied. Why are you being so stubborn?" Despite hearing this, Mother Yashoda refused to give up. She was drenched in perspiration and yet she was not deterred. Mother Yashoda became even more determined and refused to give up. She said, "I will not stop until He is tied."

The other gopis were laughing, and so was Mother Yashoda. She could not understand what was happening. "Even if I have to stay here all day, I will tie Him up," she thought. In her attempts to bind her son, Mother Yashoda became tired. She was in a state of total exhaustion. Her hair became disheveled and the decorating flowers had fallen. Her clothes also became disarrayed. When Krishna saw His mother's relentless determination, He showed her His mercy and agreed to be tied.

sva-matuḥ svinna-gātrāyā visrasta-kabara-srajaḥ
dṛṣṭvā pariśramaṁ kṛṣṇaḥ kṛpayāsīt sva-bandhane

—*Bhāg* 10. 9. 18

Because of Mother Yashoda's hard labor, her whole body became covered with perspiration, and the flowers and the comb were falling from her hair. When child Krishna saw His mother thus fatigued, He became merciful to her and agreed to be bound.

Thus ended the competition between the devotee and Krishna. Seeing His devotee's total and unalloyed dedication, Krishna had to accept defeat. In this way, Mother Yashoda was able to tie Him to the wooden grinding mortar.

One may ask - Can Krishna really be bound in this way? Sukadeva Goswami says, "Yes, because of His merciful nature, Krishna can actually be tied and bound by His devotee, *kṛpayāsīt sva-bandhane*. Krishna's merciful nature, *krpa-śakti*, prevailed and subdued all of his other *śaktis*.

evaṁ sandarśitā hy aṅga hariṇā bhṛtya-vaśyatā
sva-vaśenāpi kṛṣṇena yasyedaṁ seśvaraṁ vaśe

— *Bhāg*. 10. 9. 19

Evaṁ sandarśitā hy aṅga hariṇā bhṛtyavaśyatā— Through this *līlā*, Krishna demonstrated that He is indebted to His devotees. Indeed He can be captured by His devotee. Anyone who is truly devoted to Him can bind Him. The capacity to bind Krishna is

in every living entity but in order to do that, the living entity will have to develop the degree of devotion that Mother Yashoda has. Sukadeva Goswami said— *sva-vaśenāpi kṛṣṇena yasyedaṁ seśvaraṁ vaśe*— "The whole universe including Lord Brahma and Lord Shiva are under Krishna's control, yet He can be controlled by His devotee." This is Krishna's *sva-bhāva*, His eternal nature.

Mother Yashoda sternly told Krishna,"Stay

here! If You dare to move, I'll beat you." She asked the other gopis to keep an eye on Him. Until this point, Balaram was not there, so someone informed Balaram that His brother was tied up. Upon arriving, Balaram assumed His Sankarsana mood and strongly declared, "Who dares bind Krishna? I am Sankarsana. I am Sesha Naga. As Sankarsana, I can burn the entire universe with one breath. As Sesha Naga, I can inundate the entire Vraja with the poison coming from My one thousand hoods. Does this wrong-doer not know what I can do? Who has done this? Who tied Krishna?"

Someone told Balaram that it was Mother Yashoda who had bound Krishna. Upon hearing this, Balaram's mood changed. He was no longer like a fiery snake. He became like a timid mouse. Balaram's anger waned and He did not know what to do. Balaram saw that Krishna was crying. And Krishna, seeing Balaram, cried even more to invoke His mercy. Seeing Krishna crying, Balaram became angry again and shouted, "Who has tied Krishna? He is Narayaṇa. He is Narasimha. He is Vamana. He is Matsya. Krishna is the origin of all *avatāras*. He is everything. Who is the guilty one? I have one thousand hoods - I will burn this Vraja to the ground with the flames from My one thousand hoods!"

Looking at Balaram, Mother Yashoda sacarstically said,"Oh, I see. Krishna is the origin of all incarnations. If that is so, who then are You?" Balaram replied, "I am Lakshman. I am Sesha Naga, I am Sankarsana. I can do this, I can do that. " Mother Yashoda then said, "Do all these incarnations have to appear only in my home?" She picked up her stick and waved it threateningly at Balaram. She warned, "You had better get out of here before I beat and bind You as well!" Hearing this, Balaram ran away. All His Sankarsana power was no longer present. Mother Yashoda said, "Krishna is *bhagavān*? Indeed! He hears a cat meow and runs to me. *bhagavān* Narasimha is like this? If Krishna is *bhagavān*, then why does He need to steal *mākhan*?

Balaram ran from Mother Yashoda and went to Krishna, saying, "I told you so many times to give up this *mākhan* stealing. Did you listen to Me? You ignored My advice and now you are suffering. What can I do? If someone else had tied you, I would have taken care of it. But when *Mā* ties you, what can I do? I am helpless. What can I do to stop her? I heard that you broke the yogurt pot- why did you do that? Even if you had broken the pot, why did you not just stop at that? Instead you had to continue your mischief and make her more angry. My dear brother Krishna, I am sorry there is nothing I can do." Krishna heard this and began to cry even more.

Balaram continued, "I told you so many times to give up this stealing habit but you wouldn't listen. This serves you right. Today you are getting punished. All you can do is cry. Who can release you?" Balaram pleaded with Mother Yashoda,"Please untie Him, please untie

Him." Then He said, "Then I will untie Him. I will go and untie Him." Balaram was hoping that Mother Yashoda would relent and tell Him to untie Krishna. However Mother Yashoda did not relent. In the end, Balaram went back to Krishna and they both cried. Krishna cried because He was tied up and Balaram cried because He was helpless.

Srila Sukadeva Goswami further says:

nemaṁ viriñco na bhavo na śrīr apy aṅga-saṁśrayā
prasādaṁ lebhire gopī yat tat prāpa vimuktidāt

—*Bhāg*. 10. 9. 20

Neither Lord Brahma, nor Lord Shiva, nor even the goddess of fortune, who is always the better half of the Supreme Lord, can obtain from the Supreme Personality of Godhead, the deliverer from this material world, such mercy as received by Mother Yashoda.

nāyaṁ sukhāpo bhagavān dehināṁ gopīkā-sutaḥ
jñānināṁ cātma-bhūtānāṁ yathā bhaktimatām iha

—*Bhāg. 10. 9. 21*

The Supreme Personality of Godhead, Krishna, the son of Mother Yashoda, is accessible to devotees engaged in spontaneous loving service, but He is not as easily accessible to mental speculators, to those striving for self-realization by severe austerities and penances, or to those who consider the body the same as the self.

Though Krishna possess all possible powers; He is bound and controlled by *premā*. This bondage, however, being the most astonishing attribute of the Lord, is not a fault but a beautiful transcendental ornament in Krishna's Personality.

By His very nature Krishna is self satisfied (*ātmarāma*), yet He suffers from hunger. He automatically fulfills all of His desires (*āptakāma*), yet He is dissatisfied and desirous of *premā*. Though Krishna is the personification of peace and pure goodness, He becomes angry (*sañjāta-kopaḥ*). Krishna is the master of the goddess of fortune, yet anxiously looking hither and thither He steals butter like a beggar (*caurya-viśaṅkitekṣaṇaṁ*). Though Krishna instills fear in all through time and death, He flees in fear of Yashoda's stick (*bhaya-vihvalekṣaṇaṁ*). Though Krishna travels at the speed of mind, He is easily caught by the firm grip of His mother (*haste gṛhītvā*). Though Krishna is condensed bliss, He cries in sorrow (*prarudantam*). Though Krishna is unlimited and all-pervading, He is limited by being tied up.

By allowing Mother Yashoda to tie Him, Krishna showed that He can ultimately be controlled by the love of His devotees. Krishna desired this subordination and thus He allowed Mother Yashoda to tie Him. In this way, Krishna demonstrated that He can be totally controlled by the love and devotion of His unalloyed devotees.

mora putra, mora sakhā, mora prāṇa-pati
ei-bhāve yei more kare śuddha-bhakti

āpanāke baḍa mane, āmare sama-hīna
sei bhāve ha-i āmi tāhāra adhīna

—*Cc, Ādilīlā*, 4. 21-22

If one cherishes pure loving devotion to Me, thinking of Me as his son, his friend or his beloved, regarding himself as great and considering Me his equal or inferior, I become subordinate to him.

The Supreme Lord, Sri Krishna is never far from us. We may not feel so, but that is the truth proclaimed by the scriptures. In *Bhagavad-gītā* for example, the Lord has declared Himself to be, *suhṛdaṁ sarva-bhūtānām* (Bg.5.29), the intimate well wishing friend of all living entities. It is only for our apathy, that the Lord seems far away. We request all readers to please take heart from these narrations of Sri Damodar Lila, and make sincere efforts to establish and further your relationship with Him.

THE GLORIES OF SRI DAMODAR
Śrī Dāmodarāṣṭaka, Padma Purāṇa

Śrī Dāmodarāṣṭaka of Satyavrata Muni is very important for Gaudiya Vaishnavas. Orignally from the *Padma Purāṇa*, *Śrī Dāmodarāṣṭaka* is recited during a conversation between Narada Muni and Saunaka Ṛṣi. It is said that anyone who recites or even hears this prayer, especially in the Month of *kārtika*, will attract the eternal shelter of devotional service at the lotus feet of Sri Damodar.

namamīśvaraṁ sac-cid-ānanda-rūpaṁ
lasat-kuṇḍalaṁ gokule bhrājamanam
yaśodā-bhiyolūkhalād-dhāvamanaṁ
parāmṛṣṭam atyantato drutya gopyā

To the Supreme Lord, whose form is the embodiment of eternal existence, knowledge, and bliss, whose shark-shaped earrings are swinging to and fro, who is beautifully shining in the divine realm of Gokul, who [due to the offense of breaking the pot of yogurt that His mother was churning into *mākhan* and then stealing the *mākhan* that was kept hanging from a swing] is quickly running from the wooden grinding mortar in fear of Mother Yashoda, but who has been caught from behind by her who ran after Him with greater speed-to that Supreme Lord, Sri Damodar, I offer my humble obeisances.

rudantaṁ muhur netra-yugmaṁ mṛjantam
karāmbhoja-yugmena sātaṅka-netram
muhuḥ śvāsa-kampa-tri-rekhāṅka-kaṇṭha-
sthita-graivaṁ dāmodaraṁ bhakti-baddham

[Seeing the whipping stick in His mother's hand] He is crying and rubbing His eyes again and again with His two lotus hands. His eyes are filled with fear, and the necklace of pearls around His neck, which is marked with three lines like a conchshell, is shaking because of His quick breathing due to crying. To this Supreme Lord, Sri Damodar, whose belly is bound not with ropes but with His mother's pure love, I offer my humble obeisances.

itīdṛk sva-līlāsbhir ānanda-kuṇḍe
sva-ghoṣaṁ nimajjantam ākhyāpayantam
tadīyeṣita-jñeṣu bhaktair jitatvaṁ
punaḥ prematas taṁ śatāvṛtti vande

By such childhood pastimes as this He is drowning the inhabitants of Gokul in pools of ecstasy, and is revealing to those devotees who are absorbed in knowledge of His supreme majesty and opulence that He is only conquered by devotees whose pure love is imbued with intimacy and is free from all conceptions of awe and reverence. With great love I again offer my obeisances to Lord Damodar hundreds and hundreds of times.

varaṁ deva mokṣaṁ na mokṣāvadhiṁ vā
na canyaṁ vṛṇe 'haṁ vareṣād apīha
idaṁ te vapur nātha gopāla-bālaṁ
sadā me manasy āvirāstāṁ kim anyaiḥ

O Lord, although You are able to give all kinds of benedictions, I do not pray to You for the boon of impersonal liberation, nor the highest liberation of eternal life in Vaikuntha, nor any other boon [which may be obtained by executing the nine processes of *bhakti*]. O Lord, I simply wish that this form of Yours as Bal Gopal in Vrindavan may ever be manifest in my heart, for what is the use to me of any other boon besides this?

idaṁ te mukhāmbhojam atyanta-nīlair
vṛtaṁ kuntalaiḥ snigdha-raktaiś ca gopyā
muhuś cumbitaṁ bimba-raktādharaṁ me
manasy āvirāstām alaṁ lakṣa-lābhaiḥ

O Lord, Your lotus face, which is encircled by locks of soft black hair tinged with red, is kissed again and again by Mother Yashoda, and Your lips are reddish like the bimba fruit. May this beautiful vision of Your lotus face be ever manifest in my heart. Thousands and thousands of other benedictions are of no use to me.

namo deva dāmodarānanta viṣṇo
prasīda prabho duḥkha-jālābdhi-magnam

kṛpā-dṛṣṭi-vṛṣṭyāti-dīnaṁ batānu-
gṛhāṇeṣa mam ajñam edhy akṣi-dṛśyaḥ

O Supreme Godhead, I offer my obeisances unto You. O Damodar! O Ananta! O Viṣṇu! O master! O my Lord, be pleased upon me. By showering Your glance of mercy upon me, deliver this poor ignorant fool who is immersed in an ocean of worldly sorrows, and become visible to my eyes.

kuverātmajau baddha-mūrtyaiva yad-vat
tvayā mocitau bhakti-bhājau kṛtau ca
tathā prema-bhaktiṁ svakāṁ me prayaccha
na mokṣe graho me 'sti dāmodareha

O Lord Damodar, just as the two sons of KuveraManigriva and Nalakuvera were delivered from the curse of Narada and made into great devotees by You in Your form as a baby tied with rope to a wooden grinding mortar, in the same way, please give to me Your own *prema*bhakti. I only long for this and have no desire for any kind of liberation.

namas te 'stu dāmne sphurad-dīpti-dhāmne
tvadīyodarāyātha viśvasya dhāmne
namo rādhikāyai tvadīya-priyāyai
namo 'nanta-līlāsya devāya tubhyam

O Lord Damodar, I first of all offer my obeisances to the brilliantly effulgent rope which binds Your belly. I then offer my obeisances to Your belly, which is the abode of the entire universe. I humbly bow down to Your most beloved Srimati Radharani, and I offer all obeisances to You, the Supreme Lord, who displays unlimited pastimes.

Sri Srimad Radha Govinda Das Goswami

A Disciple of His Divine Grace
A. C. Bhaktivedanta Swami Prabhupada
Founder-*Ācārya* of the
International Society for Krishna
Consciousness

Glossary

A

Ācārya —an ideal teacher, who teaches by his personal example; a spiritual master.
Āptakāma — automatically fulfills all of His desires.
Ātmarāma — one who is selfsatisfied, free from external, material desires.
Avatār — a descent, or incarnation, of the Supreme Lord.

B

Bhagavān — the Supreme Personality of Godhead who is full with all opulences, God.
Bhakti ¬— devotion; loving devotional service for the Supreme Personality of Godhead.
Bhāva — state of being; manner of thinking or feeling; mood, temperament; affection, love; the preliminary stage of love of Godhead; also used as a technical term to describe a specific stage of mature love of Godhead.
Bhor — predawn hours.

C

Chor Mahārāja — the great thief; loving exclamation used for Lord Krishna.

D

Devas — the demigods or godly persons.
Dīpāvalī — this ceremony was observed by the inhabitants of Ayodhya, the Kingdom of Lord

Ramachandra. While Lord Ramachandra was out of His kingdom due to His 14 year's banishment by the order of His father, His younger stepbrother Bharata, took charge of the Kingdom. And the day on which Lord Ramachandra took back the charge of the kingdom and seated on the throne, this is observed as *dīpāvalī*. In India, this festival is generally celebrated very gorgeously in the month of *kārtika* by fireworks and lights.

G

Gopī — cowherd damsel.

Gokul — "community of cowherds", pasture land; assemblage of cows; the village in Vraja where Krishna was born; also used to designate the entire area of Vraja.

Goverdhan Līlās — the pastimes of Lord Krishna's lifting a sacred mountain named Goverdhan.

Gṛhastha — regulated householder life; the second order of Vedic spiritual life.

J

Jñāna — knowledge.

K

Kārtika — fourth month of Chaturmasya. This lies in the month of OctoberNovember.

Kathā — word or words spoken; discourse; topic or story; narrations about the Supreme Lord and His devotees.

Kartāla — hand cymbals used in congregational

chanting.
Kīrtana — singing in glorification of the Supreme Lord or His devotees.
Krpaśakti — the mercy potency of the Supreme Lord.

L
Lala — a name given by vraja vasis to Lord Krishna.
Līlās — pastime, sport.

M
Ma — mother.
Mākhan — butter, An edible emulsion of fat globules made by churning milk.
Matsya — the fish incarnation of the Supreme Lord.
Maṅgala — predawn hours; auspicious time.
Mathura — Lord Krishna's abode and birth place, which is near to Vrindvan. The name of the district where Vraja (Vrindvan) is located.
Mṛdaṅga — a clay drum used in congregational chanting.
Malatī — a kind of white jasmine plant.

P
Padmagandha Cows — specific cows whose milk is as fragrant as the lotus flower.
Paramatma — "supreme soul"; the Supersoul, or all pervading localized aspect of the Supreme Lord who accompanies every conditioned soul as the indwelling witness.

Pariśrama — hard labor.
Prābhava — "superiority".
Prema — love; pure and unbreakable love of God; the developmental stage of bhakti after bhāva (rati).
Premabhakti — loving devotional service unto the Supreme Lord.
Putana — a witch who was send by Kamsa to appear in the form of a beautiful woman to kill baby Krishna; she was killed by Him and granted liberation.

R
Rāsalīlās — the amorous dance of Krishna and the gopis of Vraja.
Rajoguṇa — the material mode of passion.

S
Śakti — potency, power energy.
Śaradkāla — the autumn season; this season takes away the rolling of dark clouds in the sky as well as the polluted water.
Sari — a dress worn primarily by women in India; consists of several yards of light material that is draped around the body.
Satyasaṅkalpaśakti — the power to fulfill each and every desire.
Sattvaguṇa — the material mode of goodness.
Svabhāva — one's constitution.

T

Tapasya — austerity; accepting some voluntary inconvenience for a higher purpose.
Trnavarta — a whirlwindshaped demon sent by Kamsa to kill Krishna.

V

Vaikuntha — "without anxiety"; the abode of Lord Narayana, which lies beyond the coverings of material universe.
Vātsalya — parental affection; transcendental love of Godhead in the mode of parenthood.
Vraja — Vrindavan, the land where Sri Krishna displayed His manifest pastimes five thousand years ago.
Vibhūtiśakti — the power to show or reveal Lord's opulence.
Vrajavāsīs — the inhabitants of Vrindavan.

INDEX TO SONGS AND VERSES.

A

āpanāke baḍa mane, āmare sama-hīna 38

E

ekadā gṛha-dāsīṣu yaśodā nanda-gehinī 4
evaṁ sandarśitā hy aṅga hariṇā bhṛtya-vaśyatā 32

I

itīdṛk sva-līlābhir ānanda-kuṇḍe 40
idaṁ te mukhāmbhojam atyanta-nīlair 41

K

kṣaumaṁ vāsaḥ pṛthu-kaṭi-taṭe bibhratī sūtra-naddhaṁ 7
kuverātmajau baddha-mūrtyaiva yad-vat 42

M

mora putra, mora sakhā, mora prāṇa-pati 38

N

na cāntar na bahir yasya 29
namamīśvaraṁ sac-cid-ānanda-rūpaṁ 39
namo deva dāmodarānanta viṣṇo 41
namas te 'stu dāmne sphurad-dīpti-dhāmne 42
nāyaṁ sukhāpo bhagavān dehināṁ gopīkā-sutaḥ 36
nemaṁ viriñco na bhavo na śrīr apy aṅga saṁśrayā 36

R
rudantaṁ muhur netra-yugmaṁ mṛjantam 40

S
sañjāta-kopaḥ sphuritāruṇādharaṁ 17
sva-matuḥ svinna-gātrāyā 32

T
tāṁ stanya-kāma āsādya mathnantīṁ jananīṁ hariḥ 11
tam aṅkam ārūḍham apāyayat stanaṁ 15
tām ātta-yaṣṭiṁ prasamīkṣya satvaras 22
tyaktvā yaṣṭiṁ sutaṁ bhītaṁ 27

U
uttārya gopī suśṛtaṁ payaḥ punaḥ 19-20
ulūkhalāṅghrer upari vyavasthitaṁ 20

V
varaṁ deva mokṣaṁ na mokṣāvadhiṁ vā 41

Y
yāni yānīha gītāni tad-bāla-caritāni ca 7
ye yathā maṁ prapadyante 30

ISKCON
Bhagavata Mahavidyalaya
Publications

From ISKCON Bhagavata Mahavidyalaya Publications

For enquiries related to distribution or for participating in services like transcription, translation, editing or proofreading of our books, please contact us: Website: www. ibmedu. org
Email: ibmpublications@gmail. com

Our Books in Hindi Language

- Grihasthon ke sadachar
- Harinama Diksha
- Mahabhasvarupa Srimati Radharani
- Sri Bhishma Stuti
- Bhaktvatsala Kshirchor Gopīnatha
- Bhakti yog
- Hridasvarya Sri Giri govardhan
- Putna Uddhar

Our Books in English Language

- Mahabhasvarupa Srimati Radharani
- Vrajmandal Parikrama

Sri Damodar Lila

www.ingramcontent.com/pod-product-compliance
Lightning Source LLC
LaVergne TN
LVHW041552070526
838199LV00046B/1921